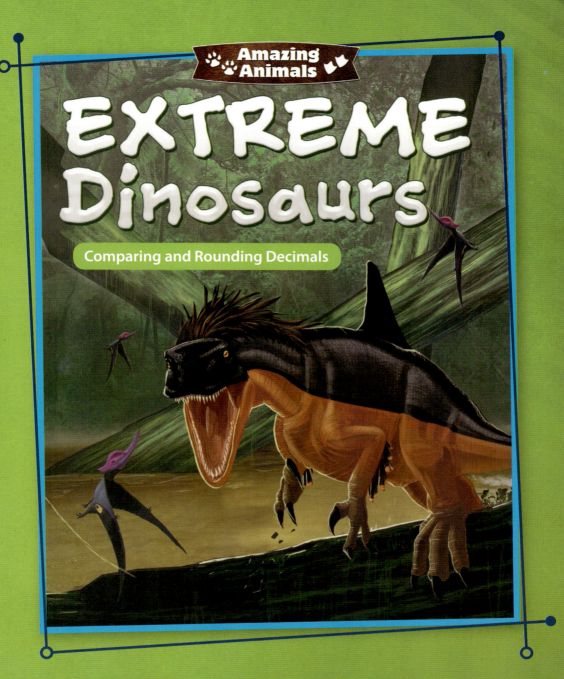

Amazing Animals

EXTREME Dinosaurs

Comparing and Rounding Decimals

Saskia Lacey

Consultants

Lisa Ellick, M.A.
Math Specialist
Norfolk Public Schools

Pamela Estrada, M.S. Ed.
Teacher
Westminster School District

Publishing Credits

Rachelle Cracchiolo, M.S.Ed., *Publisher*
Conni Medina, M.A.Ed., *Managing Editor*
Dona Herweck Rice, *Series Developer*
Emily R. Smith, M.A.Ed., *Series Developer*
Diana Kenney, M.A.Ed., NBCT, *Content Director*
Stacy Monsman, M.A., *Editor*
Kristy Stark, M.A.Ed., *Editor*
Kevin Panter, *Graphic Designer*

Image Credits: Front cover, pp.1, 5, 6, 9, 13, 14 (all), 17, 18, 20, 22–23, 24–25, 27 (top), 29 (all) illustrations by Timothy J. Bradley; pp.2–3 Vlad G/Shutterstock; p.7 Jose Maria Farfagl/WENN Photos/Newscom; p.8 Tom Wagner/Alamy; p.10 Carlos Goldin/Science Source; p.11 Lukas Barth/EPA/Newscom; p.12 Toni Albir/EFE/Newscom; p.15 Kimimasa Mayama/Reuters/Newscom; p.16 Connie Ma [flickr.com/people/ironypoisoning]; p.19 Jayne Russell/Anadolu Agency/Getty Images; p.21 National Geographic Creative/Alamy; p.26 Steve & Dave Maslowski/Science Source; all other images from iStock and/or Shutterstock.

Teacher Created Materials
5301 Oceanus Drive
Huntington Beach, CA 92649-1030
http://www.tcmpub.com

ISBN 978-1-4258-5819-3

© 2018 Teacher Created Materials, Inc.
Made in China
Nordica.112017.CA21701237

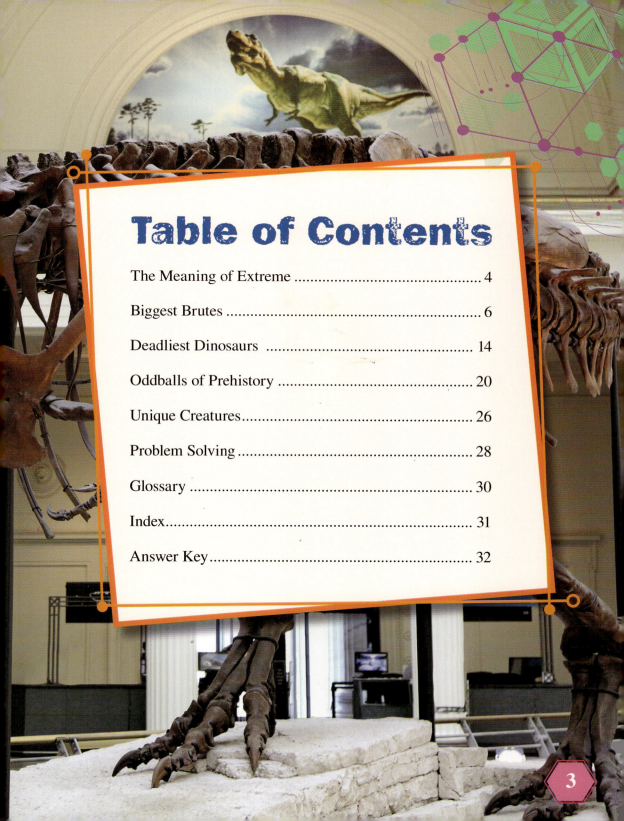

Table of Contents

The Meaning of Extreme 4

Biggest Brutes 6

Deadliest Dinosaurs 14

Oddballs of Prehistory 20

Unique Creatures 26

Problem Solving 28

Glossary 30

Index 31

Answer Key 32

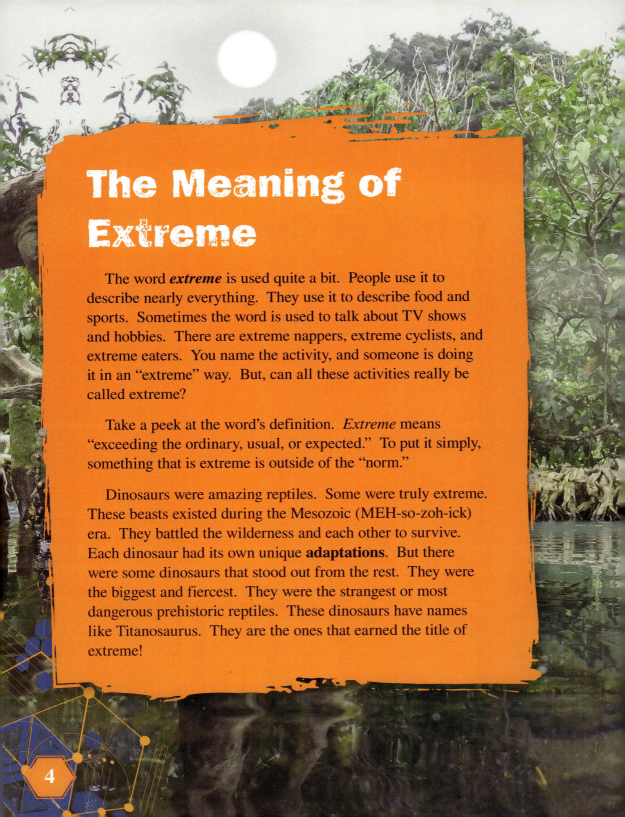

The Meaning of Extreme

The word *extreme* is used quite a bit. People use it to describe nearly everything. They use it to describe food and sports. Sometimes the word is used to talk about TV shows and hobbies. There are extreme nappers, extreme cyclists, and extreme eaters. You name the activity, and someone is doing it in an "extreme" way. But, can all these activities really be called extreme?

Take a peek at the word's definition. *Extreme* means "exceeding the ordinary, usual, or expected." To put it simply, something that is extreme is outside of the "norm."

Dinosaurs were amazing reptiles. Some were truly extreme. These beasts existed during the Mesozoic (MEH-so-zoh-ick) era. They battled the wilderness and each other to survive. Each dinosaur had its own unique **adaptations**. But there were some dinosaurs that stood out from the rest. They were the biggest and fiercest. They were the strangest or most dangerous prehistoric reptiles. These dinosaurs have names like Titanosaurus. They are the ones that earned the title of extreme!

The Spinosaurus was an extreme dinosaur because it was the only one that scientists believe lived on land and in water.

Biggest Brutes

The longest land animals in history were mighty and strong. Each of these big **brutes** earns the right to be called extreme!

titanosaurs

Titans of the Prehistoric World

The world's largest dinosaurs were plant eaters. They were part of the sauropod family. The largest and longest sauropods were from the diplodocid and titanosaur groups. Though extreme in size, titanosaurs were not **vicious** creatures.

In 2013, a new species of titanosaur was found in Patagonia. Hundreds of bones were discovered. This species may be the largest animal to ever stomp the earth. So, just how big was this **extinct** animal? It may have weighed around 70 tons (63,503 kilograms). That is the combined weight of more than 20 elephants! It was over 130 feet (40 meters) long and 65 ft. (20 m) tall. Picture a five-story building stomping around, and you can imagine how big titanosaurs were.

The titanosaur's heart might be one of its most extreme **traits**. It was a huge organ that was about 6 ft. (2 m) around—about the height of a man. With each beat, the titanosaur's heart pumped 24 gallons (91 liters) of blood.

Over the years, many reptiles have held the title of biggest ancient creature. Brontosaurus and Diplodocus are a few former titleholders. But some scientists believe that titanosaurs dwarf both those species.

Scientists believe this fossilized femur, or thigh bone, is from a sauropod.

Argentinosaurus

When talking about the biggest sauropods, this giant is bound to come up. It is known as Argentinosaurus. Some scientists think it was the largest creature to ever live. Others think that the titanosaur from Patagonia holds the title. So, who is correct? Which dinosaur was the biggest?

Well, it is hard to say. There is a problem with naming any dinosaur as the biggest. There really is not enough evidence to support such a claim. Scientists often have only **fragments** of the creatures. They discover a **vertebra** here or a leg bone there. They use these fragments to estimate the size of the creature. Of course, if new **fossils** are found of a more complete dinosaur, then experts revise their **estimations**.

An Argentinosaurus model stands tall at a museum in Germany.

So, Argentinosaurus's status as the biggest creature is still up for debate. Still, scientists are sure that it will count as one of the largest of all time.

The giant creature's bones were discovered in the late 1980s and early 1990s. A rancher in Argentina found a portion of its vertebra. The rancher thought the large bone was just a piece of wood! But a few years later, the bones were determined to be ancient.

Argentinosaurus

Argentinosaurus had pencil-like teeth. These teeth may have helped it chew leaves and other plants. Like titanosaurs, Argentinosaurus was a plant eater. Scientists believe that the dinosaur needed to consume up to 100,000 calories a day to reach its full size. That's an extreme diet!

As mentioned, the dinosaur had an extreme size, too. The creature was 115 ft. (35 m) in length. It weighed about 88 tn. (80,000 kg). With its massive body, the dinosaur would have moved slowly. It would have likely traveled only about 5 miles per hour (8 kilometers per hour).

Considering its large size, you might assume it would have a huge brain, right? Wrong! The reptile had a small brain. Experts believe that based on its small brain size, it was not as smart as other dinosaurs.

Over the years, many dinosaur fossils have been found in Argentina. Some of the fossils have been the largest ever discovered. The country is one of the world's great destinations for paleontologists. A paleontologist is a type of scientist who studies fossils. Fossils help them learn about prehistoric life.

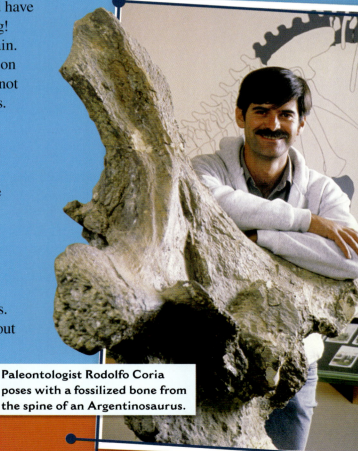

Paleontologist Rodolfo Coria poses with a fossilized bone from the spine of an Argentinosaurus.

Argentinosaurus skeleton

LET'S EXPLORE MATH

Scientists estimate that a single stride by an Argentinosaurus was about 3.658 meters long.

1. Use the equation frame to write its stride length in expanded form:

$3.658 = (\underline{} \times 1) + (\underline{} \times \frac{1}{10}) + (5 \times \underline{}) + (\underline{} \times \underline{})$

2. Which of the following place value positions completes the phrase showing how to read 3.658 correctly?

   3 and 658 _____

   A. ones
   B. tenths
   C. hundredths
   D. thousandths

This full-size reproduction of a Spinosaurus is on display at a museum in Spain.

Spinosaurus

Spinosaurus is an appropriately named dinosaur. Meaning "spined reptile," the dinosaur had long spines on its back. Each spine was 7 ft. (2 m) in length.

Like its spines, the creature was huge. It was the largest **carnivore** to ever exist. It weighed a whopping 20 tn. (18,144 kg). It measured nearly 50 ft. (15 m) in length. That is 10 ft. (3 m) longer than another famous meat-eater—Tyrannosaurus rex (T. rex).

Spinosaurus bones were first found in Egypt in the early 1900s. Since then, the reptile has been a creature of great interest. Scientists were intrigued by its unique body form. It was a land animal, but it had some of the same adaptations common to fish eaters.

Before this discovery, experts believed that some dinosaurs hunted in the water. They did not have evidence, though. Spinosaurus's fossilized bones gave them the evidence they needed.

Scientists have learned a lot from studying this dinosaur's fossils. Spinosaurus had a long jaw with nostrils at the top of its snout. This feature allowed the dinosaur to partially **submerge** its head while it swam. Yet, it could still breathe air—just like a crocodile!

Spinosaurus

LET'S EXPLORE MATH

Scientists estimate Spinosaurus's teeth were about 15.24 centimeters long.

1. Draw the number line shown above and label the missing decimals. Then, plot a point to show 15.24.

   ←|—|—|—|—|—|—|—|—|—|—|→
   15.2   15.3

2. Use the number line to round 15.24 to the nearest tenth. Explain your reasoning.

Utahraptor

Deadliest Dinosaurs

The dinosaurs with the sharpest teeth and scariest claws are the top predators of prehistory! From the famous T. rex to the equally **ferocious** Utahraptor, these are the deadliest dinosaurs of long ago.

Utahraptor

Utahraptor was discovered in the United States, in the state of Utah. That's how it got its name! It was about 20 ft. (6 m) long and as tall as an adult human. A clever beast, this raptor had a large brain compared to other dinosaurs. It had giant, powerful hind legs, too. These legs helped it chase its prey and use its "killing claw." Its long claws were one of its scariest features. On the second toe of each hind leg, the Utahraptor had a **sickle**-like claw. These claws were deadly. One swipe could slice into its prey. The creature was a vicious predator.

sickle claw

Recently, fossils of several Utahraptors were unearthed. They had been **preserved** in a block of **sandstone**. In studying these fossils, scientists hope to determine whether raptors were pack hunters. Pack hunting is where several Utahraptors work together to capture prey. Hopefully, this fantastic find will tell scientists more about the predator and its habits.

A museum visitor enjoys a Utahraptor exhibition.

Tyrannosaurus Rex

Meet Sue, the Tyrannosaurus rex. Sue was found in South Dakota in 1990. She is the most complete Tyrannosaurus skeleton ever found. Because of Sue, people have a better understanding of T. rex.

Not long ago, T. rex was thought to be the largest carnivore of prehistory. Though that is not true, T. rex still rates as one of the deadliest creatures of the Mesozoic era. Its name, which means "king of the **tyrant** lizards," says it all.

This dinosaur was not just big. It was smarter than the average prehistoric reptile. Its brain was much larger than some of its carnivorous peers. It also had better eyesight and was faster than most other meat eaters.

Experts think that T. rex was quite fast. This fierce creature likely used its speed and excellent vision to capture its prey. Its sharp, jagged teeth also helped! Each of the dinosaur's teeth were about 6 inches (15 centimeters) long. The teeth had **serrated** edges that could tear into flesh.

T. rex also had some extreme adaptations. While its hind legs were long and powerful, its "arms" were very short and strong. Some paleontologists believe that this adaptation may have helped T. rex hang onto its prey.

Sue is on display at the Field Museum in Chicago, Illinois.

LET'S EXPLORE MATH

Fossil evidence shows that T. rex had a huge skull and jaw. Use the length measurements to answer the questions.

Skull: about 1.524 meters long

Jaw: about 1.219 meters long

1. Is each length measurement closest to 1, 1.5, or 2?
2. Use >, <, or = to compare the skull and jaw lengths
   1.524 _____ 1.219

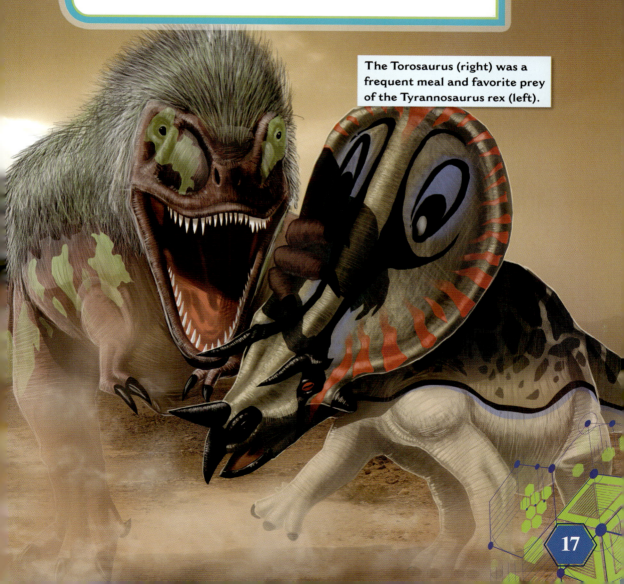

The Torosaurus (right) was a frequent meal and favorite prey of the Tyrannosaurus rex (left).

Allosaurus

The Allosaurus was 35 ft. (11 m) long and weighed 2 tn. (4,000 lbs.). During the Jurassic period, this creature was a top predator.

At first glance, this dinosaur may remind you of T. rex. The two dinosaurs share a few of the same traits. They both were **bipedal** dinosaurs. They both had large heads and strong tails that helped them balance. But, Allosaurus differs in a few important ways.

While Allosaurus had rather short front limbs, with long and sharp claws, they were nowhere near as short as those of the T. rex.

It has been suggested that the Kentrosaurus (left) and the Allosaurus (right) fought over territory during the late Jurassic period.

Allosaurus could open its jaw wider than T. rex. It had an impressive bite and a gaping mouth. This allowed Allosaurus to take huge bites of food. Its teeth were serrated and faced backward. This let it efficiently cut into its prey. That is one extreme dinosaur adaptation!

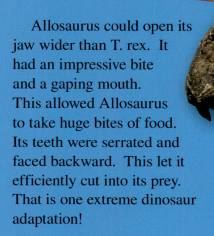

This fossilized Allosaurus skull shows its large jaw and serrated teeth.

Scientists haven't agreed on the purpose of the dinosaur's hinged and flexible jaws. Typically, the strongest bites do not start with a wide-open mouth. But it is possible that Allosaurus used its fierce teeth as a hacking weapon. It may have used its teeth to slash and bite prey. However, paleontologists have yet to find enough evidence to support this hypothesis.

LET'S EXPLORE MATH

An Allosaurus brain was about 17.8 centimeters long. Which of the following decimals and fractions are equivalent to 17.8?

- **A.** $17\frac{8}{10}$
- **B.** 17.080
- **C.** $17\frac{8}{100}$
- **D.** 17.800
- **E.** $17\frac{8}{1000}$
- **F.** 17.80

Oddballs of Prehistory

Not every dinosaur was big and scary. Some of the most intriguing dinosaurs were just plain strange. They had features and habits that may seem odd. These are the extreme oddballs of the Mesozoic era.

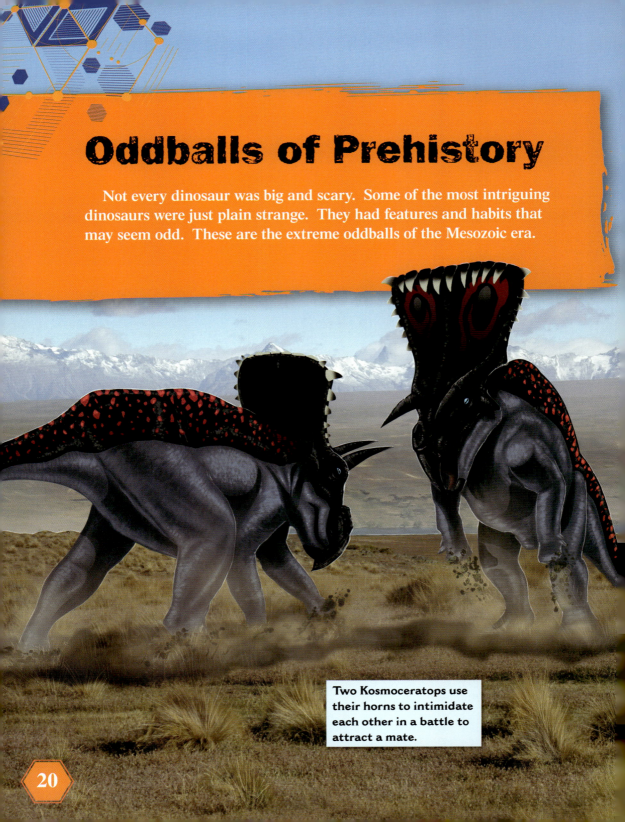

Two Kosmoceratops use their horns to intimidate each other in a battle to attract a mate.

Kosmoceratops

My, what big horns you have! Kosmoceratops was a ceratopsian, like Triceratops and Styracosaurus. Its name means "ornamented horned face." When scientists discovered its fossils, they were amazed by its skull. The head of this dinosaur is covered in horns. There are 15 horns in all! The dinosaur has horns on its nose, cheeks, and head.

The dinosaur's skull was about 6 ft. (2 m) in length. Though the creature had many horns, scientists do not think they were used for defense. It's more likely that they were for display, and they may have helped the dinosaur attract mates. Though this dinosaur may look strange, it was well adapted to its time and location.

Fossils of Kosmoceratops were first discovered in Utah. These fossils are now housed in the Natural History Museum of Utah.

A fossilized Kosmoceratops skull shows the many horns of the plant eater.

Concavenator

The Concavenator looked like a strange blend of creatures. It had a crest that was similar to a camel's hump or the fin of a large fish. The strange knobs on its forelimbs may have been feathered. The result was a truly rare beast!

Concavenator corcovatus is the dinosaur's full name. It means "the hunchback hunter from Cuenca." This dinosaur was discovered by Francisco Ortega in Cuenca (KWEN-kuh), Spain. Ortega's fossil was a rare find. The skeleton of the dinosaur was almost completely intact!

Scientists remain puzzled by the dinosaur's strange crest. They are not sure of its purpose. It might have been used to keep the dinosaur cool. Or, it might have simply been used for display, possibly to attract mates.

This dinosaur was a theropod, a part of the group *Therapoda*. Theropods were bipedal carnivores. Birds are thought to have evolved from theropod dinosaurs. The knobs of the Concavenator were similar to the structures that anchor the feathers in birds. Like its hump, scientists are not sure of the purpose of this adaptation. The knobs were too small to help the dinosaur fly! These knobs, like the dinosaur's crest, may have simply been for display.

A Concavenator chases a feathered theropod.

LET'S EXPLORE MATH

The Concavenator was about 6.096 meters long with a characteristic hump on its back.

1. Is the Concavenator's length greater than or less than 6.1 meters long? How do you know?

2. The Concavenator's raised backbones were about 39.62 centimeters taller than its other backbones. Is this greater than or less than 39.5 centimeters? How do you know?

Rhinorex

A Rhonirex is thought to have been about 30 ft. (9 m) in length. It likely weighed about 8,500 lbs. (3,856 kg). Rhinorex roamed about 75 million years ago, during the late Cretaceous period. It was a hadrosaur. This plant-eating group is known as the "duck-billed" dinosaurs because of their flat mouths that resemble duck bills.

There is no mistaking Rhinorex for another creature. Its look is truly original and unique. It is one of prehistory's strangest looking creatures.

The word *Rhinorex* means "nose king." This odd-looking feature may have been used to crush plants. Or, it may have been for display, as is the case for many strange animal features.

Rhinorex fossils were discovered in Utah in the early 1990s. But, it was not until 2014 that two paleontologists realized it was a new species of dinosaur. They found most of the skull in pieces in the Utah sandstone. They dug out all the pieces. Then, they put them together. It took about two years to do all this work!

LET'S EXPLORE MATH

A Rhinorex weighed about 4.25 tons. A modern animal, the male southern elephant seal, can weigh up to 4.4 tons. Which creature weighs more? How do you know?

Unique Creatures

The Mesozoic era was filled with strange and fierce species. There were creatures with big bellies and huge claws, such as Therizinosaurus. There were creatures like Oryctodromeus, who was known to burrow into the ground. And, there are many extreme dinosaurs still left to discover.

Scientists are learning more about dinosaurs every day. New fossils are found all the time. Information about dinosaurs can change as new fossils are found. Previous estimates and beliefs are often revised or replaced when new fossils are unearthed. New fossils can give insight that experts did not have before.

Recently, a fossilized dinosaur tail was found. But, it was not just any dinosaur tail. This tail was perfectly preserved in a lump of amber, a hard, yellow-brown substance that comes from ancient trees. Feathers and skin were clearly visible! Now, scientists have evidence that some dinosaurs had feathers. They hope to find more fantastic fossils. Such discoveries are like ancient treasure!

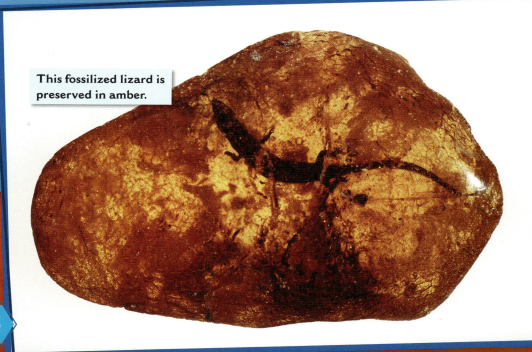

This fossilized lizard is preserved in amber.

Based on recent fossil findings in Southeast Asia, this illustration shows what a newly discovered feathered dinosaur might have looked like.

Paleontologists carefully dig a fossilized dinosaur skeleton out of rock.

Problem Solving

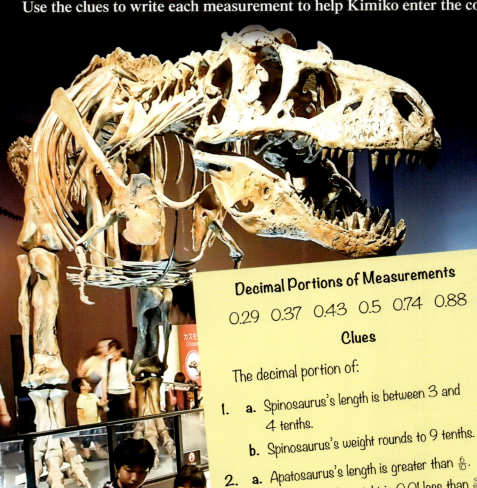

Kimiko is visiting the dinosaur fossil exhibit at a natural history museum. There is a contest to see if visitors can match the decimal portions of dinosaur measurements to clues about each measurement. Use the clues to write each measurement to help Kimiko enter the contest.

Decimal Portions of Measurements

0.29   0.37   0.43   0.5   0.74   0.88

Clues

The decimal portion of:

1. a. Spinosaurus's length is between 3 and 4 tenths.
   b. Spinosaurus's weight rounds to 9 tenths.
2. a. Apatosaurus's length is greater than $\frac{6}{10}$.
   b. Apatosaurus's weight is 0.01 less than $\frac{3}{10}$.
3. a. Argentinosaurus's length is equal to the decimal benchmark for $\frac{1}{2}$.
   b. Argentinosaurus's weight is $\frac{3}{100}$ more than 0.4.

Spinosaurus
Length: 50.___ feet
Weight: 20.___ tons

Apatosaurus
Length: 75.___ feet
Weight: 45.___ tons

Argentinosaurus
Length: 120.___ feet
Weight: 112.___ tons

Glossary

adaptations—changes in plants or animals that make them better able to live in a particular place or situation

bipedal—using two legs for walking

brutes—very large, strong creatures

carnivore—an animal that eats meat

estimations—guesses about the size, amount, or cost of something

extinct—no longer existing

extreme—exceeding the ordinary, usual, or expected

ferocious—fierce or violent

fossils—leaves, skeletons, or footprints from ancient times preserved in rocks

fragments—broken parts or pieces of something

preserved—kept in good condition over a long period of time

sandstone—a type of soft stone made from grains of sand stuck together

serrated—a row of small points or teeth along the side of the mouth

sickle—a tool with a curved metal blade and short handle often used for cutting grass or grain

submerge—to go underwater

traits—qualities that make one person or thing different from another

tyrant—someone who uses power in a cruel and unfair way

vertebra—one of the small bones linked together that forms the backbone

vicious—violent and cruel

Index

Allosaurus, 18–19

Argentina, 9–10

Argentinosaurus, 8–11, 28–29

Brontosaurus, 7

carnivore, 12, 16, 22

Concavenator, 22–23

diplodocus, 7

Egypt, 12

fossils, 8, 10, 12, 15, 21, 25–26

Kosmoceratops, 20–21

Natural History Museum of Utah, 21

Oryctodromeus, 26

Patagonia, 7

Rhinorex, 24–25

South Dakota, 16

Spinosaurus, 12–13, 28

Therizinosaur, 26

titanosaurus, 4, 6–8, 10

Tyrannosaurus Rex (T. rex), 12, 14, 16–19

Triceratops, 21

Utah, 15, 21, 25

Utahraptor, 14–15

Answer Key

Let's Explore Math

page 11:

1. 3; 6; $\frac{1}{100}$; 8; $\frac{1}{1000}$
2. D

page 13:

1.
   15.2 15.21 15.22 15.23 15.24 15.25 15.26 15.27 15.28 15.29 15.30

2. 15.2; Explanations will vary but may include that 15.24 is closer to 15.2 than 15.3 on the number line.

page 17:

1. 1.524 is closest to 1.5; 1.219 is closest to 1.
2. >

page 19:

A, D, F

page 23:

1. Less than 6.1; Explanations will vary but may include that 6.096 has 0 tenths and 6.1 has 1 tenth.
2. Greater than 39.5; Explanations will vary but may include that 39.62 has 6 tenths and 39.5 has 5 tenths.

page 25:

Male southern elephant seal; Explanations will vary but may include that 4.25 has 2 tenths and 4.4 has 4 tenths.

Problem Solving

1. a. 50.37
   b. 20.88
2. a. 75.74
   b. 45.29
3. a. 120.5
   b. 112.43